RECEIVED
09 SEP 1998
BIRDHOLME SCHOOL
S40 2EU

My Visit to the Birthday Party

Sophie Davies
and
Diana Bentley
Reading Consultant
University of Reading

Photographs by
Trevor Hill

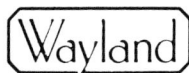

My Visit

My Visit to the Airport
My Visit to the Birthday Party
My Visit to the Dentist
My Visit to the Doctor
My Visit to the Hospital
My Visit to the Seaside
My Visit to the Supermarket
My Visit to the Swimming Pool
My Visit to the Zoo

First Published in 1989 by
Wayland (Publishers) Limited
61 Western Road, Hove
East Sussex, BN3 1JD, England

© Copyright 1989 Wayland (Publishers) Limited

British Library Cataloguing in Publication Data

Davies, Sophie
  My visit to the birthday party.
  I. Title II. Bentley, Diana III. Hill, Trevor
  428.6

ISBN 1 85210 719 7

Typeset by: Rachel Gibbs, Wayland
Printed and bound by Casterman S.A., Belgium

Contents

Hello, my name is Karan	4
We say happy birthday	6
Now we are going to play a party game	8
We play pass-the-parcel	10
I pin the tail on the donkey	12
Now it is time for tea	14
I have a piece of birthday cake	16
We play musical statues	18
Now it is time to go home	20
Glossary	22
Books to read	23
Index	24

All words that appear in **bold** are explained in the glossary on page 22.

Hello, my name is Karan.

I am going to my friend's birthday party with my brother Krishna. My friend Jonathan is seven years old today.

My Mum takes us to Jonathan's house. I have a present for him. Krishna knocks on the door.

We say happy birthday.

Jonathan and his Mum come to let us in. Most of his friends have already arrived.

We give Jonathan his birthday present. He opens it and shows all his friends. It is a game called **boules**. You play it with plastic balls. Jonathan is very pleased.

Now we are going to play a party game.

Jonathan has had lots of toys for his birthday. He shows them to me. I like this racing car best.

We are going to play **pass-the-parcel**. We sit round in a circle, and Jonathan's Mum tells us how to play.

We play pass-the-parcel.

Emma's Mum puts some music on. We pass round a parcel. Emma gives the parcel to me, and suddenly the music stops! I unwrap a layer of paper, but there are lots more layers underneath.

This time the parcel stops at Krishna. He unwraps the last layer of paper, so he wins the prize. It is a set of big felt pens.
Lucky Krishna!

I pin the tail on the donkey.

Jonathan's Mum puts a **blindfold** over my eyes so I can't see. There is a picture of a donkey, and a paper tail with a pin in it. I try to pin the tail on the donkey, but I can't find the right place. Everyone laughs. The donkey looks funny with its tail there!

Now it is time for tea.

We have a lovely tea. There are sandwiches, biscuits and crisps. Jonathan's Mum brings in his birthday cake, and we all sing 'Happy birthday to you'.

The cake has seven candles, because Jonathan is seven years old. His Mum lights the candles. He blows them out, all in one go. Now he can make a wish.

I have a piece of birthday cake.

Jonathan's Mum cuts me a piece of birthday cake. It has white icing on it. It tastes lovely.

After the cake we have jelly and cream in little paper dishes. There are special birthday cups and a birthday tablecloth too!

We play musical statues.

Now we play **musical statues**. Emma's Mum puts the music on.

We all dance to the music. When the music stops, we have to stand as still as statues. The first one to move is out of the game. Everyone looks funny standing like that! I wonder who will win?

Now it is time to go home.

Jonathan gives everyone a bag with a little present in it, to take home.

We are all going home now. We wave to Jonathan, and thank him for a lovely party. Goodbye!

Glossary

Boules A game you play with plastic balls filled with water. Each person chooses which colour balls to play with. You roll a little ball along the ground. Then you try to roll your balls as near to it as you can.

Blindfold A piece of cloth that is tied round your head to cover your eyes, so that you can't see.

Musical statues A party game. Everyone dances to music. When the music stops you must stand still. Whoever moves is out of the game. The last person still in wins the game.

Pass-the-parcel A party game. A prize is wrapped up in a parcel, with lots of layers of paper. You sit in a circle and pass the parcel round. When the music stops, the person who has the parcel unwraps a layer. Whoever unwraps the last layer wins the prize.

Books to read

Birthday Party Angela Royston (Kingfisher, 1988)
Going to a Party Anne Civardi (Usborne, 1986)
Happy Birthday – A Book of Birthday Celebrations Elizabeth Laird (Collins, 1987)
Party Games Daphne Tibbitt & Diana Underwood (Ladybird, 1982)

Acknowledgements

The author and publishers would like to thank Rivi and Karan Kent, Krishna Singh, Irene and Jonathan Card, Trisha, Emma and Jack Thompson, Ben Edwards, Jennifer Smith and Fiona James, for their help with this book.

Index

Birthday cake 14, 15, 16
Blindfold 12, 22

Candles 15

Games 8, 9, 10, 11, 12, 18, 22

Jelly 17

Musical statues 18, 19, 22

Pass-the-parcel 9, 10, 11, 22
Presents 5, 7, 20
Prize 11, 22

Tea 14, 15, 16, 17
Toys 8